GREAT LIVES

APOLINARIO *Mabini*

Dr. Stephen Latorre

Tahanan Books for Young Readers
Manila

J

Cover portrait by Yasmin Almonte

All of the pictures in this book are courtesy of the National
Historical Institute of the National Library, with the
exception of those on pages 9, 25, and 29, which are courtesy
of the Ayala Museum Library and Iconographic Archives.

Published by Tahanan Books for Young Readers
A division of Tahanan Pacific, Inc.
P.O. Box 9079, MCS Mailing Center
1299 Makati, Metro Manila, Philippines

National Library of the Philippines Cataloging-in-Publication Data
Recommended entry:
Latorre, Stephen.
Apolinario Mabini / Stephen Latorre. — Makati, Metro Manila :
Tahanan Books for Young Readers, c1992—32 p.— (Great Lives)
1. Mabini, Apolinario. 2. Heroes—Philippines—Biography.
I. Title.
DS675.8M   1992   920   P922000398
ISBN 971-630-006-9 (pbk.)

Book design and typography by ImageSetters
Printed in the Philippines by Island Graphics
3   5   4

APOLINARIO Mabini

Y ou probably have seen the picture of Apolinario Mabini many times. But perhaps you never realized who he was and why he is one of our national heroes. His face appears in the brown ten-peso bill. At the back of this bill is a drawing of the famous Barasoain Church in Malolos, the capital of Bulacan province. It is in this church where our first constitution was made, and Mabini had a lot to do with it.

Apolinario Mabini was born on July 23, 1864, in the small village of Talaga in Tanauan, Batangas, along the shores of Lake Taal. In the middle of this famous lake is Taal Volcano, the world's smallest active volcano.

Apolinario was the second child in a family of eight boys. His father, Inocencio Leon Mabini, was a poor farmer who could not read or write. His mother, Dionisia Maranan, was the daughter of the village school teacher.

The Mabini family was very poor. They lived in a small nipa hut. It was surrounded by a farm as large as a football field. In their farm they planted rice, sugar, corn, and vegetables. Mabini's mother sold their vegetables in the town market to earn money to feed her big family.

Mabini's nickname was Pule. He was very close to his mother. Dionisia was a patient, hardworking, and caring woman who wanted only the best for her children. She taught Pule how to read, write, and pray the rosary. Pule was the brightest of her children, and she wanted him to be a priest when he grew up.

Pule worked on the family farm until he was ten years old. His job was to take the carabaos to pasture. But he was a sickly boy who found farm work tiring. He preferred the company of books to the company of carabaos.

When Pule was six, he studied in his grandfather's village school. Eager to go on to high school, Mabini studied under Fr. Valerio Malabanan, a well-known priest and educator in Tanauan. In 1881 Pule won a free scholarship to San Juan de Letran College in Manila. He finished his high school studies there. While still a student he taught Latin to pay for his board and lodging.

In college Mabini was a brilliant student. He won several prizes in academic contests. He had very good study habits. A methodical student, he listened carefully to his teachers, rewriting his notes after class or at home. He had a powerful memory. It was easy for him to learn by heart a lot of facts from his books.

At first no one paid attention to Mabini. He was poorly dressed and he had strong *indio*, or native Filipino, features. At that time most of the brighter students were either Filipino Spaniards or *mestizos* (half-Spanish and half-Filipino).

One day a teacher called on Mabini to solve a difficult problem. The teacher expected the young man from Batangas to give a stupid answer that would make the class laugh. To his surprise Mabini cleverly solved the problem. He went on to excel in all his homework and exams. The teacher marveled: "Do you realize that this [Apolinario's] work comes from the mind of a brilliant man? I hope one day I will see minds like this leading our country."

Mabini's favorite subject was geography. He liked it so much that he even memorized a textbook in geography. He always got excellent grades in all subjects except Spanish literature and Spanish history. But because he was shy, he did not have many friends.

In 1882 the outbreak of a cholera epidemic in Manila and lack of money forced Mabini to return to his hometown. He worked there as an assistant teacher to his old professor, Fr. Malabanan. A year later Mabini's mother died. Mabini was heartbroken. No woman was ever closer to him than his mother. She had sacrificed much to put him through school. Mabini never courted nor married any girl.

As a teacher, Apolinario was strict but understanding with his pupils. He inspired them to study hard. He explained the lessons clearly in a strong voice. He knew how to simplify difficult problems.

His students in Batangas remembered Mabini as a quiet man. He hardly talked with them outside the classroom. He prepared his lessons well. When asking questions in class, he taught his students to go directly to the point, without beating around the bush. He also taught them the importance of religion.

Eager to further his studies, Mabini saved enough money to go back to Manila. He continued his studies in philosophy at Letran College and finished them at the University of Santo Tomas, the oldest university in the Philippines. Instead of becoming a priest, as his mother had wished, Mabini decided to become a lawyer. He graduated from law school in 1894. He was thirty years old.

At that time it was the custom for the brightest Filipino students to complete their studies in Europe. Some of them went on to study in universities in Spain or Germany. But Mabini's family was too poor to send him abroad. The Spaniards thought that the Filipinos could not govern themselves because they were poorly educated. Mabini's brilliance would later prove that a Filipino indio educated in the Philippines could handle affairs of government.

At that time the Philippine Islands was a colony of Spain. Spain was ruled by a king who was helped by parliament. Parliament made the laws of the land and the king enforced them. The rules of government which guided the king and the members of parliament were written in a basic law called the constitution.

The Philippines was ruled by a governor-general chosen by the Spanish king. But the colonial rulers abused their

A photograph of Apolinario Mabini taken around 1894

power over the indios. There were also abuses by Spanish missionaries called friars, or *frailes*. They owned large pieces of land called *encomiendas* (later called *haciendas*). The frailes used the indios to till these lands. The earnings were used to pay for the frailes's expenses and missionary activities.

While still a law student in Manila, Mabini met several bright, middle-class Filipinos who wanted the Philippines not to depend too much on Mother Spain. These young Filipinos believed that the abuses against the indios could be stopped if the Philippine Islands were changed from a colony to a province of Spain. As a province, the Philippines would have a voice in the Spanish parliament. These Filipinos formed what was called the "propaganda movement." To spread their ideas for peaceful change, or reform, they published a newspaper called *La Solidaridad*. Its editor was Marcelo del Pilar.

Mabini probably learned about the propaganda movement through a secret society called the Freemasons. Mabini had become a Freemason, a person who believed in the universal brotherhood of all men.

Many of the Filipino leaders who began the propaganda movement were also Freemasons. They used the meetings of the secret society to rally other Filipinos and Spaniards to their cause. Later on they formed a group called La Liga Filipina, or The Philippine League.

Del Pilar was the leader of the propaganda movement. He lived in Madrid, the capital of Spain. He and other Filipinos living in Spain tried to convince the Spanish parliament to pass the right laws for the Philippines. They needed someone to secretly write del Pilar about

Marcelo del Pilar, editor of *La Solidaridad*

what changes were needed in the Islands. This job was assigned to Mabini.

But life in the colony did not improve. Some leaders of the propaganda movement were arrested and thrown in prison. People began to despair. They began to think that instead of working for peaceful reform, it was better to start a war or revolution. This meant gathering an army of soldiers to fight the colonial rulers with arms to set the Philippines free from Spain.

The group that wanted total freedom from Spain formed a secret army called the Katipunan. Its leader was Andres Bonifacio. Mabini wrote to del Pilar about the Katipuneros: "They have abandoned us! They have chosen violent means instead of peaceful reforms. I hope they know what they're doing."

On August 19, 1896, someone reported the existence of the Katipunan to Fr. Mariano Gil, the parish priest of Tondo, Manila. The priest told the Spanish authorities. When the Spanish leaders got wind of a possible armed revolution, they started arresting all the suspected leaders.

Because of the discovery of the Katipunan, Bonifacio had to speed up his plans. On August 26 he called together his ragtag army of about 1,000 men. They were armed with a few rifles, some handmade pistols, *bolos*, daggers, and bamboo spears. In the hills of Balintawak, in what is now Quezon City, Andres Bonifacio and his men declared open war against Spain. It was known as the "Cry of Balintawak."

That same year Mabini came down with a very high fever of unknown cause. He was confined to the San Juan de Dios Hospital in Manila. A disease in the form of a virus had attacked his nervous system. As a result of this illness he was partially paralyzed. He could not move any of his muscles from the waist down to his toes. From that time on Apolinario was an invalid, a paralytic who could not walk but had to move around in a wheel-chair or be carried about in a stretcher. This is why he is often called the "Sublime Paralytic" in our history books. *Sublime* means someone who is very intelligent and who has many high or lofty ideas.

Because of his illness Mabini was not imprisoned by the Spanish authorities. But the other leaders of the 1896 Revolution were not as lucky. Some of them were put in prison, tortured, and killed. One of those killed was Mabini's best friend, a lawyer named Numeriano Adriano.

From his sickbed Mabini wrote a letter to the Spanish governor-general, Fernando Primo de Rivera. He said that he had not joined in the violent activities of the Katipunan. He admitted to the governor that he had helped del Pilar in running the newspaper *La Solidaridad*. He explained that he wanted peaceful reforms in the Philippines but that he did not want the country separated from Spain. Above all he did not like the Katipunan's violent use of arms and weapons to fight the government.

While recovering in the hospital, Mabini found out all he could about the goings-on of the Philippine Revolution. He reviewed the writings of Dr. José Rizal, whom he admired. Rizal was an inspiration to many followers of the Katipunan and the propaganda movement.

In the early dawn of December 30, 1896, Rizal was shot to death for treason in Bagumbayan Field (now Luneta

Park). Mabini realized deep in his heart that the struggle for peaceful reform had ended with the death of Rizal. There seemed no other path to take but to follow the way chosen by Bonifacio and his Katipuneros.

Mabini felt it his duty to continue Rizal's work of inspiring the Philippine Revolution through writing. Like Rizal, he believed in the saying: "The pen is mightier than the sword."

One day Mabini was greatly disturbed to learn from his sickbed that there was trouble within the Katipunan. Two rival groups had formed. One was led by Andres Bonifacio and his brother, Procopio. The other was led by General Emilio Aguinaldo. The Bonifacio brothers were from Tondo, Manila. Aguinaldo was from Kawit, Cavite.

The rivalry between the two groups arose, among other things, out of regional or provincial jealousies and differences. The quarrel ended with the execution of the Bonifacio brothers. Mabini later would point to this tragic incident—the failure of the Katipuneros to stay united in the face of the enemy—as one of the reasons why the Philippine Revolution failed.

Meanwhile Governor Primo de Rivera tried to stop the revolution by promising not to punish all rebels who surrendered peacefully to the government. A ceasefire, in which both sides promised not to attack each other, was agreed in the famous Pact of Biak-na-Bato. But Mabini did not believe that the pact would end the war. He did not trust the Spaniards.

Mabini left the hospital on July 5, 1897. His doctors suggested continued rest for his paralysis. He went to

Filipinos and Spaniards encamped at Biak-na-Bato, in Bulacan, to sign a ceasefire agreement.

the town of Los Baños in Laguna province. It was well-known for its soothing hot springs.

In Los Baños, Apolinario stayed with the family of General Paciano Rizal. Paciano was the older brother of José Rizal and one of the leaders of the Katipunan. Apolinario and Paciano talked of their plans about the revolution and the Katipunan.

As Mabini had predicted, the Spaniards did not keep their part of the bargain in the Pact of Biak-na-Bato. The Katipuneros who surrendered were either locked up and tortured or killed. This angered Mabini. He became even more distrustful of the Spaniards. He criticized them for not honoring their promise.

General Aguinaldo was now the leader of the Katipunan after the death of Bonifacio. Before the outbreak of the Spanish-American War, Aguinaldo sailed quietly to Hongkong where the American ships of the United States navy were anchored. In one of the American ships, Aguinaldo held a secret meeting with the Americans. They promised to help set the Filipinos free from Spain.

The promise of American help inspired other provinces to join the revolution. Katipuneros from Bulacan, Pampanga, Tarlac, Nueva Ecija, Ilocos, Camarines, and Cebu attacked their local Spanish garrisons. More people joined the Katipunan. But Mabini warned: "Let us not fool ourselves. The Americans, like the Spaniards and other European powers, covet this beautiful pearl of the Orient Seas; but we cherish its possession more, not only because God has given it to us, but because we have shed so much blood for its sake."

On May 1, 1898, the Spanish-American War reached the Philippine Islands. The war began half a world away, when the United States fought against Spain over Cuba. Because the Philippines was a Spanish colony, the Americans decided to attack it. The American ships under U.S. Commodore George Dewey fired their cannons at the Spanish ships in the battle of Manila Bay. The Spaniards were badly beaten.

General Aguinaldo returned from Hongkong to form a new government. But he needed someone who could make his position as the leader of this new government legal. This meant that Aguinaldo needed a constitution to proclaim him president of a new Philippine republic. What he needed was a good lawyer who believed in the cause of Philippine independence. Aguinaldo had heard about Mabini through Paciano Rizal and other leaders of the propaganda movement. He decided that Mabini was the man for the job.

On June 12, 1898, Filipinos gathered at Kawit, Cavite, to proclaim and celebrate their freedom from Spain. Apolinario Mabini arrived amid the festivities. He was carried by Katipunero soldiers in a hammock suspended from a bamboo pole. Aguinaldo had so eagerly awaited his arrival that he met him on the road.

Mabini's job was to organize the new government. He needed to write down laws that would work properly. The Philippines had to be recognized by other foreign countries as a new nation.

A painting of Mabini's historic meeting with Aguinaldo

From that day on, Apolinario's pen worked non-stop. He wrote the laws for the new Philippine government. His ideas shaped the document which became the future constitution of the first Philippine Republic—the Malolos Constitution. The document was named after the town of Malolos, where it was made and approved. This is why Mabini was later called the "Brains of the Revolution."

Even before the Malolos Constitution was written, Mabini's ideas were already read by Filipinos who could read and understand Spanish. His three most important works were "The True Decalogue," "The Rules of the Revolution," and "A Constitutional Program of the Republic."

Mabini taught his fellow Filipinos about love of country: "He alone possesses true patriotism who, whatever the position he fills, be it high or low, strives to do for his countrymen the most possible good."

He explained to the Katipuneros the meaning of *democracy*. Many Filipinos had never even heard of the word. It was completely new to think that power could come from the people and not from the king.

Mabini told the Filipinos to use reason and their conscience to guide them in choosing right from wrong. Before this, all Filipinos blindly obeyed what the frailes ordered them to do. He reminded them that hard, honest work would help them to prosper. Mabini wrote: "Love your God, your honor, your country, the republic. Work, develop your faculties, let no man rule you but the man you have chosen with your vote."

The officers of the revolution received many papers signed by Aguinaldo but which were written by Mabini.

Mabini became the secretary of foreign affairs and head of the first Philippine cabinet at the same time. A *cabinet* is made up of officers, each of whom heads a department needed in running the government of a country.

Mabini advised Aguinaldo to call a congress. A congress is a meeting of leaders from different parts of the country. The job of this congress was to write the constitution of the new Philippine republic. This congress met at the beautiful Barasoain Church of Malolos, Bulacan. On January 21, 1899, the Malolos Constitution was signed by Aguinaldo. Aguinaldo became the president of the first Republic of the Philippines.

The Malolos Congress met at Barasoain Church to create the constitution of the first Philippine Republic.

While American troops were busy trying to occupy Manila, diplomats from Washington, D.C. went to Paris to negotiate peace with Spain. This meeting was called the Treaty of Paris. It was here where Spain sold to the United States the right to rule the Philippine Islands for a sum of 20 million dollars. Aguinaldo, Mabini, and the other Filipino leaders were angered and saddened by this news. The Americans indeed had betrayed Aguinaldo as Mabini had feared. This was the start of the Philippine-American War.

The Spaniards had surrendered Manila to the American forces before Aguinaldo's rebel army could capture the city. The American troops were bigger in number and had better weapons than the Philippine army. Because the Filipinos failed to take Manila, they were forced to

The Treaty of Paris allowed for Spain to sell the Philippine Islands to the United States for 20 million dollars.

American and Spanish forces clashed at the battle of Manila.

retreat up north to hide in a heavily forested area, in what is now Caloocan City.

Little by little the American forces pushed the retreating Filipinos northwards. In March 1899 they captured the town of Malolos. Aguinaldo's troops fled to Pampanga, then to Tarlac and finally to Pangasinan.

Because of his illness, Mabini could not escape with the retreating rebel army. The Americans wanted to capture Mabini, the "Brains of the Revolution." Mabini had to go into hiding. With the help of his brothers and a few soldiers, he was carried in a hammock to a small town called Cuyapo in Nueva Ecija province.

Mabini hid in the house of the family of a certain Zacarias Flores. The entire province of Nueva Ecija was

A painting of Mabini being carried across a river during the Philippine-American War

already in American hands and Mabini was on the wanted list. A spy told the American soldiers where Mabini was hiding. He was captured and brought by train to Manila.

Mabini was imprisoned in Fort Santiago from December 11, 1899, until September 23, 1900. He continued to write in his prison cell. This time he attacked the new colonial masters of the Filipinos, the Americans.

More painful to Mabini than imprisonment was to learn that some Filipino leaders and members of the Malolos Congress had sided with the Americans. They wanted the Philippines to become another state of the United States of America. These men visited Mabini in his prison cell to ask him to join their cause.

In this painting Mabini is taken into American custody after he was captured in Nueva Ecija.

Mabini refused. He insisted that he would never give in to the Americans. He believed that what the Filipinos needed was the right and power to rule themselves. He never wavered in his belief that the Philippines must be free from *any* kind of foreign rule.

Mabini also complained about being persecuted and spied upon by the Filipinos who were supporting the Americans: "What makes me suffer more than the cruel sickness which has been shortening my life is seeing some of our countrymen on the side of the Americans. Many of them are occupying highly paid jobs shameful for a Filipino to occupy. Under their orders, they send men to spy on me day and night."

Mabini at the police station in the Walled City of Intramuros, where he was imprisoned

Mabini was released from prison in September 1900. He continued writing, this time with more vigor. He lived in a small nipa hut in the Nagtahan district of Manila, located along the banks of the Pasig river. Today the house stands as a museum in honor of Apolinario Mabini. It is found inside the compound of Malacañan Palace, the house of the President of the Philippines.

Mabini wrote articles for the local newspapers, harshly criticizing the new American rulers. He urged the Filipino soldiers never to surrender to the Americans.

With the Filipino rebels in retreat, the United States government sent a military governor to rule the Islands. His name was General Arthur MacArthur. He asked the captured Filipino rebel leaders to respect the flag of the United States of America. Among those he tried to persuade were three Generals—Artemio Ricarte, Maximo Hizon, and Pio del Pilar; and Apolinario Mabini. All four refused to swear allegiance to the American flag.

General MacArthur decided that these troublemakers had better be sent far away. As prisoners in Manila they gave hope to the Filipino soldiers still holding out in the mountains and forests of the island of Luzon. Mabini and the three generals were exiled to Fort Asan, a prison camp in the island of Guam, outside the Philippines.

On January 15, 1901, Mabini and his friends boarded the U.S. ship *Rosencranz* bound for Guam. Mabini's life in exile lasted two years. His brother Prudencio was allowed to accompany him as his nurse.

Being a prisoner and an exile was not a problem to a bright man like Mabini. He could still work with his

General Arthur MacArthur, who banished Mabini to exile in Guam

mind. He even found time to study how to read and write in English. More important, he wrote down his ideas about why the Philippine Revolution failed in his political masterpiece, *The Rise and Fall of the Philippine Republic.*

He wrote: "Our country is passing through a critical stage. The loyal Filipinos will have a terrible end. It is not because the enemy is greater, but because of the corruption and treason of our countrymen. They hesitated on the way and are selling us for a handful of gold."

Mabini considered himself a man of letters and read a lot in his lifetime. But as a writer, he was never at home with literature, poetry, and the arts. In his writings he sounded always like a lawyer arguing a case. That is why almost all of his letters are formal in nature. They reveal little about Mabini the man. He did not write too many personal letters.

Mabini was a man of mystery. He remained for the most part in the shadows, much like a puppet master who pulled the strings of the Katipunan army. In the same way he was the "power behind the throne," quietly guiding the actions of President Aguinaldo and his cabinet and the whole Malolos Congress.

In Guam, Apolinario Mabini, feeling perhaps that he would not live long, feared that he might die a man without a country. He wanted so much to return to his beloved Philippines. Some Filipinos who had befriended the new American rulers tried to bring him back to the Philippine Islands. Other exiles in Guam had already been allowed to return just by swearing to the flag of the United States of America. Mabini finally gave in. He only asked his American captors to allow him to do it on Philippine soil and not in Guam. He returned home on February 26, 1903, on the U.S. ship *Thomas*.

Mabini was offered money and a high government position by the new American colonizers. But he chose to retire from public life. He lived quietly in his nipa hut along the Pasig River to finish the book he began in Guam. He also wrote articles for the local newspapers. He believed he could help educate his people on how to govern themselves.

In 1903 a big cholera epidemic struck Manila. This time Mabini caught the deadly disease. He died on May 13, 1903, barely three months since his return from exile.

Mabini's funeral was attended by many friends and admirers. Important government officials, Filipinos and

Mabini's nipa hut in Nagtahan

Americans, led the thousands who bade him farewell. A twelve-horse carriage carried his coffin through the streets of Manila. Foreign and local newspapers praised him as a great hero of the Filipino nation.

Apolinario Mabini was only 39 years old when he died. He did not die on the battlefield, like our other heroes. Instead he died in bed of a dreaded disease. But he died a hero because of how he lived.

Mabini did not allow his crippling illness to stop him from serving his country. He worked hard for reforms under the Spanish government. He used his great intellect to lay the legal foundations of the first Philippine revolutionary government. Above all, he never stopped asking the Filipino people to carry on the bitter struggle

A bronze statue of Mabini inside the National Library Compound in Manila

for independence. Nearly a century later, his words survive today to remind us of the great cost a nation must pay for its freedom:

"… Let us fight while a grain of strength is left us; let us acquit ourselves like men, even though the lot of the present generation is conflict and sacrifice. It matters not whether we die in the midst or at the end of our most painful day's work; the generations to come, praying over our tombs, will shed for us tears of love and gratitude, and not of bitter reproach."

Bibliography

Primary sources:

Craig, Austin. *Filipinos' Fight for Freedom* (Filipiniana Reprint Series). Mandaluyong, Metro Manila: Cacho Hermanos, Inc., 1985.

Kalaw, Teodoro. *Las Cartas Politicas de Mabini.* Manila: Bureau of Printing, 1935.

Mabini, Apolinario. *The Rise and Fall of the Philippine Republic* (Filipiniana Reprint Series). Mandaluyong, Metro Manila: Cacho Hermanos, Inc., 1985.

Palma, Rafael, *La Revolucion Filipina por Apolinario Mabini.* Manila: Bureau of Printing, 1931. 2 vols.

Secondary sources:

Agoncillo, Teodoro A. and Alfonso, Oscar M. *History of the Filipino People* (Rev. Ed.). Quezon City: Malaya Books, 1972.

Guerrero, Leon Ma. *We Filipinos.* Manila: Daily Star Publishing Co., 1984.

Henares, Hilarion Jr. "Apolinario Mabini: Anti-American," in *Sun and Stars Alight*, 1976.

Joaquin, Nick. *A Question of Heroes.* San Juan, Metro Manila: Filipinas Foundation, Inc., 1977.

Laya, Juan C., et al. "Apolinario Mabini," in *Philippine Adventure*, vol. II, 1962.

Majul, Cesar Abid. *Apolinario Mabini: Revolutionary.* Manila: National Heroes Commission, 1964.

del Rosario, Maria Salud, et al. "Si Apolinario Mabini" in *Masayang Pook ng Maiikling Talambuhay*. Manila: Philippine Book Company, 1962.

About the Author

Dr. Stephen Latorre is a regular columnist of two leading dailies published in Manila. He earned a masters degree in history and philosophy from the University of Navarre in Pamplona, Spain. A *cum laude* graduate of the University of the Philippines, he is currently serving on the faculty of the U.P. Department of European Languages.

Dr. Latorre has written several books on religion, including *Guidebooks for Baptism and Confession* and *Catechism of Catholic Doctrine*. This is his first biography for young people.

The author lives in Alabang, Metro Manila.